Autism
and *A Workbook for Adolescents and Adults*
Depression

Katie Saint, PhD, LPC, BCBA-D and Carlos Torres, BS

AUTISM AND DEPRESSION

A Workbook for Adolescents and Adults

All marketing and publishing rights guaranteed to and reserved by:

FUTURE HORIZONS INC.

(800) 489-0727

(817) 277-0727

(817) 277-2270 (fax)

E-mail: info@FHautism.com

www.FHautism.com

ISBN: 978-1-949177-46-6

INSTRUCTIONS

Depression is very common, but can sometimes be difficult to recognize. Forty percent of adults and twenty percent of children and teenagers with an autism spectrum disorder (ASD) have a depression diagnosis (Greenlee, Mosley, Shui, Veenstra-VanderWeele, and Gotham, 2016). Individuals with ASD are four times more likely to experience depression than neurotypical individuals; this is why regular screening is important. Additionally, rates of depression are higher in individuals with ASD with higher intelligence (Hudson, Hall, and Harkness, 2018).

It is important to look for signs and symptoms before depression becomes a more serious issue. Symptoms of ASD can sometimes mask depression symptoms, so it's valuable to know what to look for.

The following symptoms are warning signs that depression could be an issue:

- Increased rigidity in routines outside the norm for the individual
- Negative comments about self or about not having a need for friends; rationalizing negative perspectives.
- Increased avoidant behavior (completely ignoring, making excuses, increased argumentative communication, etc.)
- Social withdrawal and/or withdrawal from interest(s)

The following symptoms could be misinterpreted as depression but may just be a characteristic of ASD:

- Change in mood
- Tone of voice not matching the situation
- Resistance to activities
- Low social motivation

This workbook discusses how to treat symptoms of depression and increase skills that lead to a meaningful life. Symptoms of depression often ebb and flow. This workbook is helpful during times of depressive states, and also for maintaining positive, healthy behaviors. This book can be used independently or as a group therapy tool as a way to identify meaningful goals to keep the user self-motivated as they move toward their ideal self. Goals can be monitored individually or with another person.

The strategies in this book are based on behavior analytic principles. Acceptance and commitment therapy (ACT) is a behavior analytic tool that has been effective in reducing symptoms of depression and anxiety and in increasing skills. ACT works to identify what people value most, then increases the frequency of those value-related behaviors by pairing them with available short-term and long-term reinforcers, which address motivation problems (Gould, Tarbox, and Coyne, 2017). ACT is effective in helping people learn to respond to their emotions in a way that leads to a more meaningful life, and increases distress tolerance as well as impulse control (Lomas, Medina, Ivtzan, Rupprecht, and Eiroa-Orosa, 2018).

ACT helps clients tolerate non-preferred activities by showing them how those activities help them achieve what they truly want (O'Hora and Maglieri 2006; Castro, Rehfeldt, and Root, 2016). ACT defines behaviors that lead to increased depression and anxiety, and identifies barriers to work through (Hayes, Strosahl, Bunting, Twohig, and Wilson 2005). ACT is also effective in increasing self-awareness, which helps to fight depression caused by behaviors people were not aware of (Barnes-Holmes, Hayes, Dymond, and O'Hora 2002).

ACT therapy has helped thousands of people worldwide, and it is not just treatment for people with an autism or depression diagnosis. These strategies are helpful for everyone!

WHY USE THIS BOOK?

Let's be honest. The tactics in this book are going to require work, and you are going to have to do things that may cause you anxiety. Why should you waste your time? What is in it for you other than the obvious answer of "to decrease depression?"

There is a saying, "There is no such thing as a free lunch." This saying means that nothing we want in life comes for free. I am guessing, you are opening this book because you have experienced pain and disappointment. Your life isn't what you want it to look like. You believe your life could be better, but things you have tried in the past didn't really work— or maybe they worked at first, but then quit working.

To answer the question "what's in it for me?" please consider the following questions:

1. If you didn't have depression, how would you act differently?
2. How would not having depression impact your free time?
3. How would it impact the way you talk to yourself and take care of yourself?
4. What would you no longer do?
5. What would you do more of?
6. What would you have more of socially, emotionally, or physically?
7. What would you start doing?
8. What new goals would you set, and what would you achieve?
9. Why would getting rid of depression improve your life?

Please take a moment to pause and consider these questions. The answers to these questions can serve as motivation to push through hard times where you feel unmotivated, discouraged, or otherwise down.

Please remember we would never expect you to be a good weight lifter, basketball player, surgeon, or professional video game player just by reading a book. We actually need to practice the skills in order to get results. If you are feeling hesitant reading this, please know we will walk you through barriers related to self-doubt, self-discipline, and motivation. A more satisfying life can be achieved.

DEPRESSION SYMPTOM CHECKLIST

In this section, we would like to work on self-awareness of problematic symptoms related to depression and autism spectrum disorder. The following symptoms are commonly associated with depression. Go through and describe what your experiences have been like with these symptoms. Identifying these symptoms will help us create a treatment plan for you! Answer based on how often you have experienced these symptoms in the last month.

1. Feelings of sadness/hopelessness/irritability most of the day. Describe for each emotion:

_____

_____

_____

What triggers these feelings?

_____

_____

_____

Is there a time of day that triggers this?

_____

_____

_____

Decreased interest and/or enjoyment in activities you used to enjoy.

Describe:

_____

_____

_____

2. Trouble sleeping and/or sleeping too much.
Describe:

_____

_____

_____

3. Low energy and/or increased restlessness.
Describe:

_____

_____

_____

4. Feelings of worthlessness/negative thoughts/excessive guilt, etc.
   Describe:

   _____

   _____

   _____

5. Difficulty concentrating, focusing, and completing or starting tasks.
   Describe:

   _____

   _____

   _____

6. Thoughts of suicide or self-harm.
   Describe:

   _____

   _____

   _____

TRAITS COMMONLY ASSOCIATED WITH AUTISM

Certain traits of autism can help people succeed in life, such as having a great memory! Other symptoms can cause difficulties if not shaped into a more productive behavior. The list below is taken from the DSM-5 diagnostic (American Psychiatric Association, 2013) criteria for autism spectrum disorder. Take this assessment to identify the symptoms you could benefit from working on. Accurate self-reflection can be very difficult, so discuss this list with a trusted person. Please note that having autism can be a strength. This book is not trying to alter an autism diagnosis, but rather explore if there are any areas that could be contributing to depression.

Ability to connect with others

❑ I have a lot of close friendships that I can connect with.

❑ I struggle to find people who I can talk to, but I have some.

❑ I don't have any people who I can be open with.

Communication

❑ It is easy for me to express how I am feeling and why.

❑ I can express how I am feeling, but not why.

❑ It is very hard for me to express my thoughts and feelings.

Reading other people's verbal and non-verbal communication

❑ It is easy for me to accurately read what other people are thinking and feeling.

❑ Sometimes I can accurately read what other people are thinking and feeling.

❑ It is hard for me to accurately read what other people are thinking and feeling, and sometimes this causes problems for me.

Repetitive behavior

❑ I do not have any repetitive behavior that causes difficulties in my life.

❑ At times, my repetitive behavior can cause stress or problems in my life.

❑ My repetitive behavior causes significant stress and problems in my everyday life.

Insistence on sameness

❑ I am open to new experiences and am able to quickly adapt to unexpected changes.

❑ I sometimes struggle with change, but can eventually adapt.

❑ Unexpected change is extremely stressful for me.

Restricted interests

❑ I have a variety of interests and plenty of leisure activities to fill my time.

❑ I tend to stick to a few interests but still have a variety.

❑ I have only one or two interests that I am willing to spend my time doing.

Sensory

❑ Sound, sight, touch, and taste do not typically cause stress in my life.

❑ Sound, sight, touch, and taste sometimes cause stress in my life, but I can adapt.

❑ Sound, sight, touch and taste cause significant stress and limitations in my life.

EVALUATION OF TRIGGERS

In this section, we would like to work on self-awareness related to events or triggers that increase your struggles. Knowing the triggers you struggle with is important, so you can problem solve how to respond to or avoid your triggers. Discuss each of these questions with a therapist or a trusted friend/family member and brainstorm how to work through these triggers.

Sensory experiences can sometimes make achieving goals more difficult. Additionally, having restricted interests can limit life if you are not willing to expand beyond those interests. People with an autism diagnosis often are detail oriented and can pinpoint exactly what may trigger them and how it affects them. If this is communicated, it can be very helpful for problem solving around any sensory issues. Exposure and practice can make sensory issues less of a factor.

What causes me to struggle most?

_____

_____

_____

What sorts of situations make me anxious?

_____

_____

_____

What sorts of situations make me feel most uncomfortable?

_____

_____

_____

HYGIENE

Good hygiene has been shown to increase mental health, whereas poor hygiene has been shown to decrease mental and physical health (Kurer, Watts, Weinman, and Gower, 1995). Additionally, bad hygiene can hurt people socially. Use this section to evaluate how you are doing with your hygiene habits.

How often do I shower?

How often do I brush my teeth?

How often do I have body odor in front of others?

Do I apply deodorant daily?

What aspects of my appearance may help social interactions with people (including posture and facial expressions)?

What aspects about my appearance may hurt social interactions with people (including posture and facial expressions)?

How do others view me based on my appearance?

How does my hair help or hurt my appearance?

What habits do I have that might gross people out or make them uncomfortable (such as picking nose, biting fingernails, having long fingernails, etc.)?

After self-reflecting on my hygiene, do I feel like there are any behaviors I need to change related to how I take care of myself? If so, list here:

IDENTIFYING EXPERIENTIAL AVOIDANCE

We tend to avoid things we don't like. However, we often make our lives worse when we avoid things. To be successful in every area of life, we need to endure some uncomfortable moments. It is important to evaluate if you are avoiding things you need to face.

The purpose of this section is to increase your awareness of experiential avoidance. Experiential avoidance is behavior we do that is counterproductive to our health, values, and goals. The following questions will help you to evaluate if you are participating in experiential avoidance. Ask a trusted individual for their insight, to gain additional perspective; it is common for people to struggle with accurately perceiving themselves due to misinterpretations of how others may or may not view them.

It is also common for people to make generalizations based on their initial experience, and this may sometimes lead to experiential avoidance. The generalization may be helpful if it was a good experience, but hurtful if it was a bad experience. If someone had a bad experience that individual could heavily focus on the negative ramifications that took place physically or mentally. This can serve as an obstacle for growth because someone may be less likely to have an open mind when revisiting the same or a similar situation. This is why it is important to label experiential avoidances: so the client can learn how to overcome those obstacles.

What are my eating habits like? Eating too much, too little, or foods that are bad for you can make emotional regulation more difficult.

❑ I eat too much or too little per day.

❑ I eat too much sugar.

❑ I eat too much junk food.

❑ Other: _____

Do I abuse any substances? Abusing substances is a common way for people to sabotage personal goals, and often abusing substances increase depression and anxiety.

❑ Alcohol

❑ Cigarettes

❑ Prescription abuse

❑ Caffeine

❑ Other: _____

What are my sleeping habits like? Poor sleeping habits can lead to health issues, motivation issues and emotional regulation issues.

❑ Too much sleep

❑ Too little sleep

❑ Inconsistent asleep and awake time

❑ No bedtime routine

Leisure Time

Leisure time can be a form of experiential avoidance if it is blocking you from your goals and causing you to not deal with your emotions. Leisure time can also be very healthy. This section is to help evaluate if your leisure time is helping you or hurting you.

What do I do for fun?

How often do I contact people for leisure activities?

How often do I leave the house for social reasons?

How flexible am I when spending time with peers?

How good of a listener am I? What is an example of how I am a good listener?

_____

_____

What would my friends say about me?

_____

_____

How would my family describe me?

_____

_____

What are new things I have tried? (Refusing to try new things often leads to isolation and rigidity, which increases depression and anxiety.)

_____

_____

_____

Do I have people I consider close friends, and would they describe me the same?

_____

_____

_____

What should I be doing to help my life, but I am not doing?

How does this affect the progress on my goals?

What will make/tempt me to start doing the avoided task?

What tasks am I avoiding, making it more difficult to meet my goals?

How do I adapt to change?

To increase awareness of your everyday activities that help or hurt you, please fill out the schedule below that reflects your typical day.

Centers for Disease Control and Prevention (2019) recommends seven to ten hours of sleep per night for young adults. The amount of time spent on healthy leisure activities varies depending on personal responsibilities, but should never prevent you from meeting basic needs: hygiene, school, work, or social obligations. For example, hitting snooze four times at six AM moved you away from your values because it lead to you being late for work.

	Healthy (helps moves you toward your values)	Unhealthy (moves you away from your values)
6 AM		
7 AM		
8 AM		
9 AM		
10 AM		
11 AM		

	Healthy (helps moves you toward your values)	Unhealthy (moves you away from your values)
12 PM		
1 PM		
2 PM		
3 PM		
4 PM		
5 PM		
6 PM		
7 PM		
8 PM		
9 PM		

	Healthy (helps moves you toward your values)	Unhealthy (moves you away from your values)
10 PM		
11 PM		
12 AM		
1 AM		
2 AM		
3 AM		
4 AM		
5 AM		

What are some things that you don't like, but you need to do anyway to reach your goals?

_____

_____

_____

IDENTIFYING YOUR PRIORITIES

Now that you have worked on some self-awareness regarding areas of struggle, we would like to help you identify what you truly care about. Identifying what you truly care about makes it easier to prioritize your actions and gives you a path to follow that will lead to increased life satisfaction. Being out of line with our values leads to depression and anxiety (Hayes, Strosahl, Bunting, Twohig, and Wilson, 2005).

Having specific goals is instrumental to achieving success and improving mental health! If we are not intentional about who we want to be and what we want our life to look like, we will drift and give in to our impulses. A good goal is measurable, specific, and achievable.

1. Based on the previous assessments, what are the top areas you feel like you would benefit from working on?

_____

_____

_____

2. If you didn't struggle in those areas you identified, how do you think your life would improve? What would that look like?

_____

_____

_____

3. What has worked in the past to bring you joy?

_____

_____

_____

4. What causes you the most stress in your day to day life?

_____

_____

_____

5. What would a perfect life look like to you?

_____

_____

_____

6. What would have to change in order for you to achieve that perfect life?

_____

_____

_____

7. Write out three specific behaviors you need to do less of to help achieve your ideal life:

_____

_____

_____

8. Write out three specific behaviors you need to do more of to help achieve your ideal life:

_____

_____

_____

GOAL-SETTING TOOLS AND RESOURCES

Visuals are often helpful for giving you a map of what to expect. Below, we created visuals and activities to outline the processes you might go through, and to help you increase self-awareness during your journey.

The "pathway to success" visual is intended to motivate and educate about what long-term progress might look like. Feeling better is not a straight path, there may be bumps along the way. Pushing through these difficult times is the hardest part of feeling better! Motivation may be low and anxiety levels may be high. It is this stage that often blocks people from overcoming their struggles in order to become successful. That is why pushing through those emotions is critical.

The "depressive cycle" image is meant to display a common cycle people get stuck in that prevents healing and growth. The visual is meant to be used as a reminder of what not to replicate throughout your treatment.

DEPRESSIVE CYCLE VISUAL GOAL-SETTING WORKSHEET

Write your goal in the "goal" box. Write an action you did (positive or negative) to affect the progress of the goal. Circle if that action helped or hurt the progress of your goal. In the "feelings" box, describe the emotion(s) you felt after completing the above action. If you are unsure if an action helps or hurts a goal, reach out to a safe person to talk through your progress.

GOAL:

Help/Hurt	Help/Hurt	Help/Hurt

ACTIONS:

FEELING:

IDENTIFYING SUPPORT SYSTEMS

Working on achieving goals is hard, and it is important not to do it alone. Research supports you are more likely to achieve your goals if you involve other people (Abad, Fearday, and Safdar 2010). This section is to help you identify who your support systems are.

List names and contact info for people you could call in an emergency:

_____

_____

_____

List names and contact info for people who you could contact to talk if you are stressed out:

_____

_____

_____

List names of people who would be willing to hold you accountable and give you honest feedback to help keep you on track with your goals. It is okay you are naming the same people.

_____

_____

_____

DATA COLLECTION

Daily Goal Data Sheet

Tracking your progress helps hold you accountable and increases your self-awareness of your progress. You can use our data sheets or create your own. This will become a fun visual to display your progress.

	Sun	Mon	Tue	Wed	Thu	Fri	Sat
Goal 1:							
Goal 2:							
Goal 3:							

Why is it worth meeting these goals?

What techniques did I use to reach these goals?

Weekly Goal Data Sheet

	Week 1	Week 2	Week 3	Week 4
Goal 1: _____ _____ _____				
Goal 2: _____ _____ _____				
Why is it worth meeting these goals? _____ _____ _____				
What techniques did I use to reach these goals? _____ _____ _____ _____ _____				

INCREASING THE FEEL-GOOD CHEMICALS

This section focuses on the chemicals in your body that can be a barrier to progress if you do not have enough of them. Dopamine is a chemical in your body that makes you feel good, motivates you, and fights depression (Koob, 1996). Certain activities can help you produce dopamine. Use these questions to help figure out healthy ways you can increase dopamine production.

1. Exercise produces dopamine. List types of physical activities that you would be willing to do to help your body feel better:

_____

_____

_____

2. Healthy relationships produce dopamine. List behaviors that would help you to develop closer friendships:

_____

_____

_____

3. Doing things that line up with your values produces dopamine. List activities you can do on a daily basis that line up with your values. Examples could include reading books, spending time with family, or joining game groups.

_____

_____

_____

4. When you notice that you are struggling, it is helpful to do two-minute value activities. Even two minutes of doing a value-based activity can encourage dopamine production. List activities that take two minutes or less that relate to your values. For example, if you value health and music, you could do push-ups and listen to a song.

5. Write an example of a daily schedule that would include the activities listed above:

SELF-REFLECTION ON CONSEQUENCES

Part of why people don't achieve their goals is because they are not aware of how their choices are impacting them (Howell and Buro, 2011). When people become more aware of themselves and how their choices impact them, they tend to make better choices. Being self-aware is a skill that needs to be developed and practiced. That is why so much of this book includes self-reflection.

Fill this chart out to reflect on how you are doing with moving toward your values.

	Area of Life	Values Statement	What do I do that helps me move toward this value?	What do I do that leads me away from this value?	What is the next step I should take to move closer to my value?
EXAMPLE	**Friendship**	*I want to have close friends.*	*I text with my friends.*	*I often blow off hanging out.*	*Schedule a time to hang out that I don't skip.*
	Family				
	Work				
	Friendship				
	Leisure				
	Romantic Relationships				
	Other:				

MOOD EVALUATION

This section discusses how we respond to emotions. Emotions can be a huge barrier to progress; our actions can affect our moods. Research supports that we cannot avoid our feelings (Hayes, Strosahl, Bunting, Twohig, and Wilson, 2005). If we attempt to, it increases the duration and intensity of those emotions. Finding a way to face our emotions is critical to our future success.

Here is a list of ways you can face your emotions. Check the ones you would be comfortable with. Keep in mind that if you are not comfortable with any of the ideas on this list, it is important you come up with different healthy and effective ways to process your emotions.

- Talking to a friend about your emotions
- Journaling about your emotions
- Recording yourself talking about your emotions
- Singing about your emotions
- Playing a musical instrument
- Drawing
- Other _____

Here is a list of counterproductive ways to respond to emotions. Check the ones that you sometimes use. Recognizing unhealthy ways you deal with emotions can help you to stop those habits and improve your relationships.

- Acting grumpy to friends or family
- Eating or drinking to feel better emotionally
- Watching movies or playing video games to shut off your brain and avoid feelings
- Sleeping instead of facing your emotions
- Shopping to avoid your feelings

- Investing in unhealthy relationships
- Isolating yourself to avoid uncomfortable feelings
- Other _____

Reflect on the past week. Use the chart below to reflect on how you are responding to your moods.

Mood	Response
Tired	*Head down, no eye contact, avoidance of activities*

EXAMPLE

Now, rewrite your moods from the past week and write a healthier response that would help you move toward your values despite your emotions.

Mood	Response
Tired	*Positive body language, use of self-regulation tools, engage with others*

EXAMPLE

How can you help yourself choose the healthier response to your moods next time they occur?

_____

_____

_____

BARRIERS

A lot of times, we have good reasons for not achieving our goals. It is important that you identify any reasons you have experienced that have become an obstacle for achieving what you want. In life there are often internal or external barriers that get in the way of reaching your goals. Internal barriers are how we feel physically or emotionally. External barriers are things outside of our body that get in the way of our goals, like money or other people. Being aware of your barriers can help you to face them and problem-solve around them.

Use the chart on the next page to identify and work through your barriers.

EXAMPLE

Barrier	How can I accept it as something I need to do to achieve my goal?	How do I need to problem-solve around it?	Benefit
I get a lot of anxiety when I am in groups.	I need to recognize that many people feel anxiety in groups. If can't endure being in groups, I will not be able to hold down a job or attend social events, which are important to me.	To deal with the anxiety I feel in groups, I need to have a safe person with me, to remind myself of what I will gain from facing my fear, and to have time to myself to relax afterward.	Attending group activities that I enjoy and building relationships.

ACCEPTANCE

A huge part of success and happiness is accepting that we cannot escape all the bad things in life. In fact, sometimes bad things lead to amazing things! Bad experiences increase the value of our good experiences. We must be aware that if we want something, we need to accept the bad that may come with it. This perspective can help us endure the things we may not enjoy (Gould, Tarbox and Coyne, 2017).

List what you value and then what unpleasant or uncomfortable things you will need to accept in order to have that.

	Value	Things I need to Accept: Example One	Things I need to Accept: Example Two
EXAMPLE	*Having friends*	*Listening to stories I don't care about*	*Playing games that aren't my favorite*

APPRECIATING THE GOOD

Increasing our awareness of the good things happening to us is so important to our mental health. Often, we downplay the good things in life and focus on the bad. We often say really negative things about ourselves, and very little positive. Each and every person has value. Each and every person has reasons why they can feel good about themselves. Teaching ourselves to notice the good can help us feel better about life. This worksheet is intended to help you get in the practice of noticing the good.

	Sun	Mon	Tue	Wed	Thu	Fri	Sat
Something I did I am proud of							
Something I appreciate							
Something hard I worked through							

Self-esteem is something many people struggle with, and can make depression worse. It's important to build your self-esteem by completing small achievable goals, and purposely putting yourself in situations where you can succeed. If you don't know what your strengths are, ask a trusted individual to help you discover them. It is also important to remember that we all struggle with certain things and have room to grow. Accepting that no one is perfect is an important part of building your self-esteem.

List three situations where it would be easy for you to succeed.

Example: When I work on computers, I feel confident and effective because I have success with diagnosing the problem and finding a solution.

1. _____

2. _____

3. _____

PROBLEM THOUGHTS

We all have thoughts that get in the way. Self-doubt creeps in and it tells us we are not good enough, people won't like us, and we will fail. We won't ever get those thoughts to completely go away. Those thoughts are part of being human, but we can train ourselves to not let them control our behavior. Step one is being aware of them, and step two is figuring out what strategies work for you to decrease their power (Castro, Rehfeldt, and Root, 2016).

When you are about to do something important or something you care about, what thoughts come to mind? List them here and mark whether they are helpful or hurtful.

Thoughts	Helpful	Hurtful
I can't do this.		X
This is going to be hard, but it's worth it.	X	

EXAMPLES

STRATEGIES FOR DISMISSING UNHELPFUL THOUGHTS

Defusion is the ACT therapy term for addressing your thoughts and emotions. A better definition of defusion is "the ability to distance yourself from your thoughts and feelings and let them come and go, rather than being caught up in them or controlled by them (Russ, 2011)." Defusion strategies help you to be the boss of your thoughts and emotions.

1. **Look at the evidence.** Sometimes we have thoughts that are not backed with any evidence. It can help us dismiss them if we look at the actual evidence.

Thought	Evidence	What would other people say?	True/Not True
EXAMPLE No one likes me.	I was invited to two social events this month.	My coworker tells me that I am fun to hang out with.	Not True

2. **Change the "but" to an "and."** Sometimes our thoughts come up with excuses for why we shouldn't do things that we value. When we catch ourselves doing this, we can change the "but" to an "and" to help us see that we can still push through, despite what is going on inside. List some statements you have made that can be switched.

	Excuse/Thought	Changed Statement	Benefit of Pushing Through
EXAMPLE	**But** I can't go to the party, I am bad at making friends.	I am bad at making friends, **and** I am going to the party to work on it.	I move toward my goal of making friends.

Questions to ask to defuse thoughts:
1. Is this thought a fact?
2. Is this thought someone else's opinion?
3. Have I based my thought on someone else's opinion, a fact, or my own opinion?

4. What situations support my opinion? Do I have enough evidence?

5. Does my rigidity influence the validity of thought?

6. What is the expectation or social norm related to my thought?

7. Can I tolerate or dismiss this thought?

8. What could be worse or better about this thought?

9. Am I over-analyzing the situation?

10. Are my emotions or insecurities blinding me?

11. What do my safe people think about the validity of this thought?

PERSPECTIVE-TAKING ACTIVITY

Throughout your day, positive and negative situations will arise. These situations might make you feel a certain way (good or bad), but there will always be a situation that could make you feel better or worse. Constantly thinking about the bad situations you're in could lead to depressive thoughts, while focusing on the positive only may lead to overconfidence issues and may come off as arrogant. Perspective-taking is very important to gain a healthy perspective on each situation you are in. Considering how something could be worse can help a person feel better about a situation and view it as not as big of a deal. Considering how something could be better serve as motivation for achieving new goals.

	What Could Be Worse?	Event/Thought	What Could Be Better?
EXAMPLE	I offended a girl by being awkward and she refused to talk to me.	I was awkward in front of a girl I have a crush on, but she talked to me.	I made her laugh at a joke.

EMOTIONAL REACTION MAPPING

This worksheet can be used to evaluate if your emotional response was appropriate for the situation. Often, people have emotional reactions that are not appropriate for the situation and this can make the situation worse.

	Event	Thought	Emotion	Behavioral Representation of the Emotion or Thought	Was that Reaction Helpful or Hurtful?
EXAMPLE	Example: Lost in the first round of a video game tournament	I am the worst and can't beat anyone	Anger, sadness, defeated	Stormed off, pouted, made comments about other players/friends	Hurt my relationships, made it less likely to be invited back

SKILL DEVELOPMENT ACTIVITIES TO FIGHT DEPRESSION

This section is designed to work on skill deficits that can sometimes lead to feelings of depression and anxiety. Building a strong skill set in the below target areas will create more opportunities to thrive in your everyday environment, reducing symptoms of depression.

Go through each section and practice the skills with a trusted partner. Ask for honest feedback and ideas to create more success.

Ability to Connect with Others

Connecting with others is important; not having solid friendships commonly leads to depression (Whitehouse, Durkin, Jaquet, and Ziatas, 2009). The ability to connect with others is vital for your mental health.

To work on developing the ability to connect with others, you must practice this skill.

Practice Steps:

Step 1. Put yourself in social situations at least one to three times per week.

- Find activities of interest in your area
- Attend activities individually or with familiar/trusted people
- Portray a positive attitude, even if you are nervous
- Attempt to have conversations with people at the activities
- Come up with topics of conversation that would be appropriate for the context

Step 2. Read other people's tone of voice, facial expression, and body language, and then adapt your behavior to it.

- Watch TV shows and analyze, with a friend or family member, what people's tone of voice, facial expression, and body language mean.
- After being in a social situation, analyze (with a trusted friend) what

the tone of voice and body language of the other person meant in the previous interaction.

Step 3. Be mindful of your non-verbal communication.

- Practice your tone of voice, facial expression, and body language in a mirror.
- Ask trusted individuals for feedback on your facial expression, tone of voice, and body language.

Step 4. Have good listening skills.

- Practice listening to other people's interests/stories.
- Make sure to ask follow-up questions.
- Make sure to show interest with your tone of voice, facial expression, and body language.
- Ask trusted friends or family for feedback.

Based on the steps above, list your action plan:

A. What goals do you have for yourself?

_____

_____

_____

B. What activities will you practice to reach your goals?

_____

_____

_____

C. How will you track your goals?

D. How will you reward yourself for making positive progress in your goals and, ultimately, accomplishing your goal?

E. What barriers do you expect would make this goal challenging? What are some ideas to get around this barrier?

F. What feedback have friends or family given you on your friendship skills, tone of voice, facial expression, and body language?

COMMUNICATION

The number one reason couples go to counseling is because of communication problems. Communicating how you feel and maintaining relationships can be hard. If communication is something you struggle with, it could impact your friendships. Poor communication can also impact your employment and ruin job interviews. This is a very important skill to work on.

How to Effectively Communicate

How we communicate impacts our relationships and our ability to meet our needs. There are multiple ways to communicate each message you want to convey. To practice this skill, write out a statement and practice saying it in three different ways, changing your tone of voice, body language, and facial expression.

Statement: _____

_____

_____

Present the message in a way that could be offensive or harmful.

   Example: Leave me alone! (No eye contact, mad or sad facial expression and body language.)

Present the message in a way that would be helpful to you and your relationship.

   Example: My dog passed away this morning. I am really upset about it. Would you mind if we talked in a little bit? (Maintain eye contact and a soft tone of voice that is not showing anger or frustration with the other person.)

Present the message in a way that might be neutral. Note that even neutral communication can sometimes be hurtful.

Example: Would you mind giving me space for a few minutes? I had a really bad day. (Maintain eye contact and use direct, limited body gestures.)

List here how you will practice working on this skill:

1. _____

2. _____

Increasing Conversation Skills and Listening Skills

It is important to be able to hold meaningful conversations with people. This is what develops friendships and creates a sense of connection. Responding with one-word answers or only talking about your interests can lead to people not talking to you and relationships breaking down. Being a good listener is critical to friendships; if you are not a good listener, it could hurt or end your friendship.

Reading the following tips and then practice discussing another person's interests. Try to maintain the conversation for at least ten minutes.

- Find topics for conversation that could relate to the person you are talking with.
- Observe how the other person may be feeling about the conversation by reading their non-verbal cues.
- Engage in back-and-forth conversation.
- Ask follow-up questions to show interest and clarify statements that might be misleading or confusing.
- While listening, show interest by nodding your head in agreement or to show understanding.
- React with an emotion that correctly correlates to the emotion the speaker is displaying.

- While listening, maintain eye contact and non-verbal, affirming that you care about what the person has to say.
- Having a beginning, middle, and end to stories.
- Make sure the point of your story is clear and do not ramble on.

Sarcasm and Friendly Teasing

Sarcasm and friendly teasing is a common way people connect. Being able to evaluate your audience is very important: sarcasm and teasing could be really offensive if done in the wrong context. It's important to recognize when the mood, person, location, and topic of conversation determines when and if it's okay to joke.

Sarcasm is when people try to be funny or ironic by saying something that they do not actually mean in a dry tone of voice. Sarcasm can hurt relationships when the listener is unaware that sarcasm is being used, or if sarcasm is used in the wrong context.

Friendly teasing occurs between friends or family and is meant to be funny, not hurtful. Forms of friendly teasing would be followed up with non-verbal or verbal communication validating the statement was intended to be a light-hearted joke rather than an offensive statement.

To work on developing joking/sarcasm skills, write a list of three different friends or family members and list what you could (and could not) joke about with them, and why.

Example:

Person: Mom

Okay to joke about: Mom's bad cooking

Why? Even though this would be insulting to some people, mom finds it funny and not offensive. I know this is true because she often jokes about it, as well.

Not okay joke about: Mom's weight

Why? Mom clearly feels bad about her weight and has made comments that she is insecure about how she looks.

Person 1

Okay to joke about: _____

Why? _____

_____

Not okay to joke about: _____

Why? _____

_____

Person 2

Okay to joke about: _____

Why? _____

_____

Not okay to joke about: _____

Why? _____

_____

Person 3

Okay to joke about: _____

Why? _____

_____

Not okay to joke about: _____

Why? _____

_____

Reading Other People's Verbal and Non-Verbal Communication

The ability to read people's tone of voice and non-verbal communication is a critical part of interacting and relationships. If you are missing non-verbal cues, you could interpret conversations incorrectly and cause harm to your relationships. Misinterpreting non-verbal communication sometimes results in viewing situations more negatively than they really are. These issues can lead to a negative self-image, and to thoughts that can possibly lead to depressive symptoms.

Take some time to watch some drama TV shows, and pause the show to analyze what the non-verbals mean in the given moment. Do this with a person who is really good at reading non-verbals, so they can give you feedback. Only use shows with real people (not cartoons).

Write what you learned about analyzing non-verbal communication from the TV show:

_____

_____

_____

Ask a trusted person who will give you honest feedback on your non-verbals. List feedback you were given of things to work on:

_____

_____

_____

How does your facial expression impact conversation?

_____

_____

Based on the previous activities, list how you will work on your non-verbals throughout the week:

Based on the previous activities, list how you will work on reading other people's non-verbals throughout the week:

How will you get feedback on your communication skills, so that you know if you are improving?

What is expected (facial expression, tone of voice, body language, distance away from speaker) when someone shares difficult (sad, defeated, angry, insecure, traumatic) information?

RIGIDITY

Being rigid in your routines and daily life can lead to isolation, and problems can arise due to inflexibility. Having restricted interests can really limit your friendships and job opportunities. If you feel like you can only be friends with people who are exactly the same as you, you are not likely to have very many friends. To develop friendships, you often have to try new things and be open to other people's interests. Compromise is a big part of friendship.

At times, routine and rigidity can be productive. Not all rigidity should go away: for example, morning and nightly routines or the assembly of something at your place of employment. There are things that need to be done a certain way, but you may have to be creative when something unexpectedly changes that could throw off your normal routine (waking up late or early, emergency situations, etc.). Even though your normal routine may be more efficient, problem solving and creative thinking will help you in times of crisis.

How to identify if you have a rigidity problem:

- You will not compromise on how things get accomplished
- New things are a challenge
- Schedule changes or cancellations are difficult to regulate
- Conflict arises in your relationships due to you resisting change

Cost Analysis:

Ask a trusted individual to help you evaluate what your rigidity has cost you.

How will you get feedback on your repetitive behaviors, so that you know if you are improving?

How has your rigidity hurt your relationships?

How could (or how has) your rigidity hurt your employment or potential employment?

How has your rigidity limited your leisure activities or hurt your chance at gaining new leisure skills? Are there activities or events you have missed out on? Do you get bored or into trouble in your free time due to lack of activities?

How has your rigidity hurt your daily living situation or health?

How does your rigidity impact your emotions? Has being over- or under-emotional about a problem or topic ever ruined a day or an event?

Why is it difficult to recover once your emotions escalate?

_____

_____

_____

Does your rigidity prevent you from being considerate to others, or from considering how other people might be feeling?

_____

_____

_____

How to Become More Flexible and Reduce Rigidity

Work on exposing yourself to situations that are outside of your comfort zone by intentionally breaking routines and trying new activities. Remind yourself that change and flexibility are part of life and relationships, and to motivate you to push through your discomfort, remember the costs of rigidity. Be open to creative problem solving solutions, and set specific goals for yourself. Surround yourself with safe people who can help you feel more comfortable in new situations. Choose to practice expanding your flexibility when you have extra time and the emotional stability to self-regulate.

List activities you will commit to practicing to work on your flexibility:

1. _____

2. _____

3. _____

How to Find New Interests

- Set goals
- Consult friends on the different interests they have, and ask how to get involved
- Search the internet for groups in your area
- Visit your local library and explore a hobby or leisure section

List new activities you can try to work on your flexibility:

1. _____

2. _____

3. _____

List any barriers that would make it difficult for you to be flexible:

_____

_____

List the potential solutions to those barriers:

_____

_____

Behavior change is hard. Are there are any tools or resources you need to add to your life in order to hold yourself accountable while working on these changes? Write how you will motivate and hold yourself accountable:

_____

_____

SENSORY

Having sensory issues can limit where you go, how you communicate, and how you respond to certain circumstances. Being aware of your sensory issues and coming up with strategies to cope with them will help you to explore more places and to feel more confident socially.

Practicing exposure can improve many sensory issues. There are three different types of exposure therapy that have been proven to be effective at reducing sensory problems (Busscher, Spinhoven, Van Gerwen, and de Geus, 2013): systematic desensitization, exposure therapy, and flooding.

Systematic desensitization consists of taking extremely small steps to work up to your goal. This method is used to desensitize people to things that cause them a lot of stress or anxiety. With each step, you would increase the difficulty, and would slowly reach your ultimate goal while causing the least amount of stress or anxiety. Each step could take many repetitions before you become comfortable in completing the given task. Do not move on to the next step until you can do the current step with low levels of anxiety. When you are working on exposure, it is very important to try and make it a positive experience.

Try to limit your systematic desensitization plan to nine steps or less; it could be too overwhelming to complete steps in the double digits while competing with symptoms of depression. Adaptations can be used to make each step more tolerable, leading to success. Examples of adaptations for sensory issues could include headphones for noise sensitivities, gloves for touch sensitivities, and sunglasses for visual sensitivities. Other adaptations can be used that dull the sensory experience. To completely overcome sensitivities, fading the adaptations is important.

Here is an example of what the steps could look like if putting lotion on makes you uncomfortable.

1. Simply hold the lotion bottle in your hands.

2. Put one drop of lotion on your finger and immediately wash it off.

3. Put one drop of lotion on your finger and leave it on for fifteen to thirty seconds, then wash it off.

4. Put one drop of lotion on your finger and leave it on for one minute, then wash it off.

5. Rub lotion into a two-inch area and leave it on for approximately thirty seconds.

6. Put a small dot of lotion on your hand and leave it on.

7. Put enough lotion on to cover two inches of your hand and leave it on.

8. Put enough lotion on to cover one full side of your hand and leave it on.

9. Final Goal! Put enough lotion on to cover both sides of your hand and leave it on.

Consider if you would benefit from systematic desensitization. Use the worksheet below to write out your own steps to help document your success in reaching your goal.

Systematic Desensitization Worksheet

List the steps you will take to reach your final goal.

1. _____

2. _____

3. _____

4. _____

5. _____

6. _____

7. _____

8. _____

9. Final Goal! _____

Exposure therapy is the practice of getting full exposure to a situation that makes you uncomfortable. This is another proven strategy that helps people overcome sensory issues or other fears/anxieties. People choose exposure therapy instead of systematic desensitization if they want faster results, or if they know they can practice getting exposure without it ruining the rest of their day.

If a person had an aversion to lotion were practicing exposure therapy, they would need to use the lotion once a day with a supportive or safe person around. That safe person would encourage them, remind them of their coping skills, and try to help make it a positive experience.

Flooding is a less common exposure therapy. Flooding consists of getting an extremely high level of exposure to a dislike. You would be exposed to your sensory aversion repeatedly until you no longer had a stress response to the sensory experience.

If you wanted to use flooding to address lotion aversion, for example, you would put lotion on large portions of your body once per hour until you no longer felt an aversion.

Before picking which treatment method to use, it is important to identify if sensory issues are a problem or not. Here are some questions to determine if they are an issue or not:

How does your sensitivity prevent you from doing something you enjoy?

_____

_____

_____

How does your reaction to the sensitivity cause you stress or embarrassment?

_____

_____

_____

How does this sensitivity impact your relationships with your family/ friends? Does it ever cause conflict?

_____

_____

_____

Please list any sensory issues you want to overcome, and which method you feel would be best successfully overcome the issue.

Example:

Sensitivity: Putting lotion on hands

Treatment Method: Systematic desensitization

Reason for Treatment Method: Lotion causes a high level of anxiety, and full exposure would cause too much anxiety.

Sensitivity: Tolerating large groups

Treatment Method: Exposure therapy

Reason for Treatment Method: I can handle group exposure, even though it's stressful, if I'm with safe people and use coping tools.

Sensitivity: _____

Method for Treatment: _____

Sensitivity: _____

Method for Treatment: _____

Sensitivity: _____

Method for Treatment: _____

REASSESSMENT

Depression Symptom Checklist

Now that you have gone through each chapter, it is time to re-evaluate how you are doing! At the beginning of the book, we asked you to answer these questions based on how often you have experienced these symptoms in the last month. Now, answer the questions again and compare your answers.

Feelings of sadness/hopelessness/irritability most of the day.
Describe:

_____

_____

_____

Decreased interest and/or enjoyment in activities you used to enjoy.
Describe:

_____

_____

_____

Trouble sleeping and/or sleeping too much.
Describe:

_____

_____

_____

Low energy and/or increased restlessness.
Describe:

_____

_____

_____

Feelings of worthlessness/negative thoughts/ excessive guilt, etc.
Describe:

_____

_____

_____

Difficulty concentrating, focusing, and completing or starting tasks.
Describe:

_____

_____

_____

Thoughts of suicide or self-harm.
Describe:

_____

_____

_____

Goal Reflection

List the goals you have met through the course of this book:

1. _____

2. _____

3. _____

List the benefits of meeting the above goals.

1. _____

2. _____

3. _____

List the strategies you will use to maintain your progress.

1. _____

2. _____

3. _____

TROUBLESHOOTING

If you made it all the way through this book and are still struggling, there are a couple of questions to ask yourself.

- Did I practice the strategies discussed in each chapter multiple times per week?
- Did I have support from others as I worked on self-reflection and accountability?
- Would I benefit from going through this book with a trained therapist?
- Would I benefit from talking to my doctor about my mental health?

We hope this book was an encouragement to you, and that it led to you moving closer to your values and responding well to your emotions. Life is a journey, and we all need to work on continual improvement in order to live happy and fulfilling lives.

REFERENCES

Abad, C., Fearday, A., & Safdar, N. (2010). Adverse effects of isolation in hospitalised patients: a systematic review. *Journal of hospital infection*, 76(2), 97-10

American Psychiatric Association. (2013). *Diagnostic and statistical manual of mental disorders* (5th ed.). Arlington, VA.

Barnes-Holmes, D., Hayes, S. C., Dymond, S., & O'Hora, D. (2002). Multiple stimulus relations and the transformation of stimulus functions. *In Relational Frame Theory* (pp. 51-71). Springer, Boston, MA.

Busscher, B., Spinhoven, P., van Gerwen, L. J., & de Geus, E. J. (2013). Anxiety sensitivity moderates the relationship of changes in physiological arousal with flight anxiety during in vivo exposure therapy. *Behaviour research and therapy*, 51(2), 98-105.

Castro, M., Rehfeldt, R. A., & Root, W. B. (2016). On the role of values clarification and committed actions in enhancing the engagement of direct care workers with clients with severe developmental disorders. *Journal of Contextual Behavioral Science*, 5(4), 201-207.

Centers for Disease Control and Prevention. (2019). How much sleep do I need? Atlanta, GA: US Department of Health and Human Services. Retrieved from https://www.cdc.gov/sleep/about_sleep/how_much_sleep.html

Hayes, S. C., Strosahl, K. D., Bunting, K., Twohig, M., & Wilson, K. G. (2005). What is acceptance and commitment therapy? In S. C. Hayes & K. D. Strosahl (Eds.), *A Practical Guide to Acceptance and Commitment Therapy* (pp. 3–29). New York: Springer Science-Business Media

Howell, A. J., & Buro, K. (2011). Relations among mindfulness, achievement-related self-regulation, and achievement emotions. *Journal of Happiness Studies*, 12(6), 1007-1022.

Hudson, C. C., Hall, L., & Harkness, K. L. (2018). Prevalence of depressive disorders in individuals with autism spectrum disorder: A meta-analysis. *Journal of Abnormal Child Psychology*, https://doi.org/10.1007/s10802-018-0402-1

Gould, E. R., Tarbox, J., & Coyne, L. (2017). Evaluating the effects of Acceptance and Commitment Training on the overt behavior of parents of children with autism. *Journal of Contextual Behavioral Science*, 7, 81-88.

Greenlee, J. L., Mosley, A. S., Shui, A. M., Veenstra-VanderWeele, J., & Gotham, K. O. (2016). Medical and behavioral correlates of depression history in children and adolescents with autism spectrum disorder. *Pediatrics*, 137(Supplement 2), S105-S114.

Koob, G. F. (1996). Hedonic valence, dopamine and motivation. *Molecular psychiatry*, 1(3), 186-189.

Kurer, J. R. B., Watts, T. L. P., Weinman, J., & Gower, D. B. (1995). Psychological mood of regular dental attenders in relation to oral hygiene behaviour and gingival health. *Journal of Clinical Periodontology*, 22(1), 52-55.

Lomas, T., Medina, J. C., Ivtzan, I., Rupprecht, S., & Eiroa-Orosa, F. J. (2018). A systematic review of the impact of mindfulness on the well-being of healthcare professionals. *Journal of Clinical Psychology*, 74(3), 319-355.

O'Hora, D., & Maglieri, K. A. (2006). Goal statements and goal-directed behavior: A relational frame account of goal setting in organizations. *Journal of Organizational Behavior Management*, 26(1/2), 131–17.

Whitehouse, A. J., Durkin, K., Jaquet, E., & Ziatas, K. (2009). Friendship, loneliness and depression in adolescents with Asperger's Syndrome. *Journal of Adolescence*, 32(2), 309-322.

AUTHOR BIOS

CARLOS TORRES, BS. Carlos is a published author, coach, and behavior treatment therapist. He is the program director for a young adult program that helps adults with disabilities gain independence. He creates curricula and designs groups to develop social skills, vocation skills, leisure skills, and relationship skills. Additionally, he coaches special needs sports teams for the Miracle League of Wisconsin. Carlos has a degree in special education. He dedicates his time to help at-risk children and young adults gain skills for independence.

KATHERINE SAINT, PhD, LPC, BCBA-D. Katherine has her doctorate in behavior analysis and is a licensed professional counselor. Katherine presents locally and internationally on topics related to autism, mental health, and behavior analysis. Katherine has a private practice focusing on mental health counseling, and is the director of training at an applied behavior analysis program that helps people with disabilities. Katherine has designed college courses as well as published books and articles related to mental health.

CPSIA information can be obtained
at www.ICGtesting.com
Printed in the USA
JSHW050834180721
16913JS00001B/1